For Raf, the lover of the deer, on his second birthday, from Grandpa

This book teaches 5 basic woodland animals and is intended for toddlers from 1-4 years

Baby Bear
loves woodland animals...

by Mark Dorgan

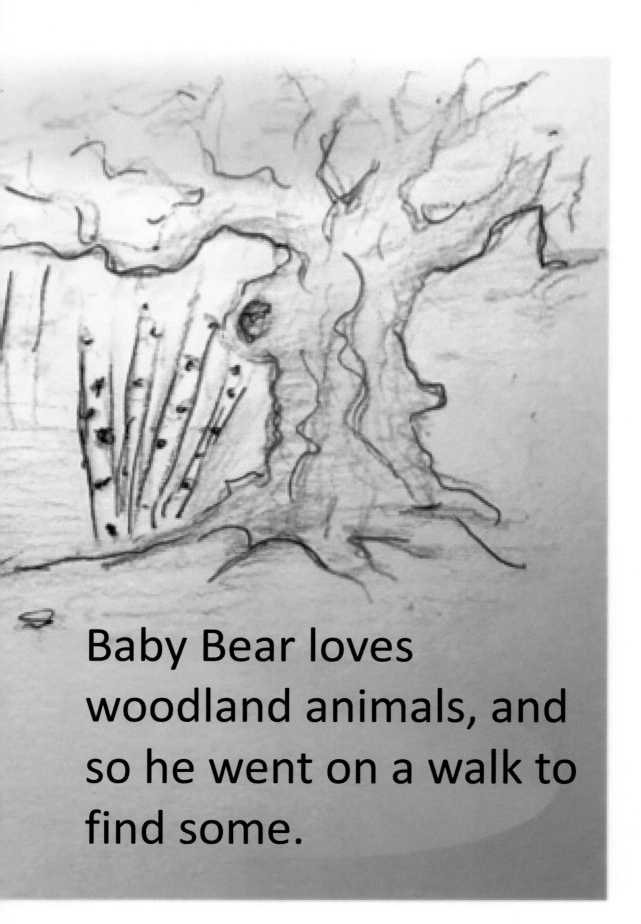

Baby Bear loves woodland animals, and so he went on a walk to find some.

He found a red fox...

...some squirrels
playing in the
sunshine by a pool...

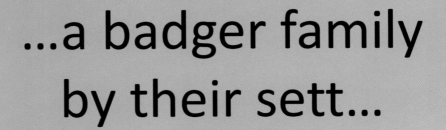

...a badger family
by their sett...

...and a daddy deer,
a stag, in the grass.

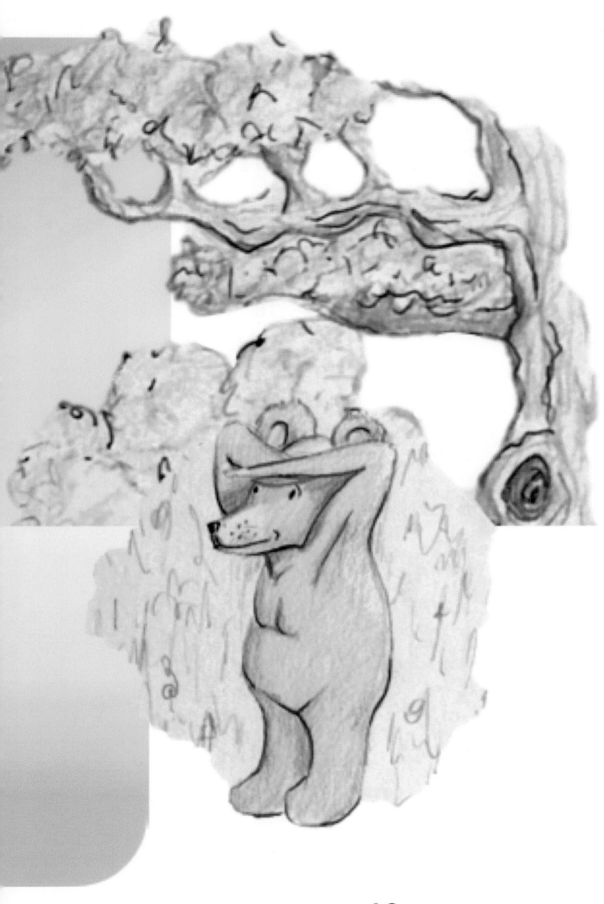

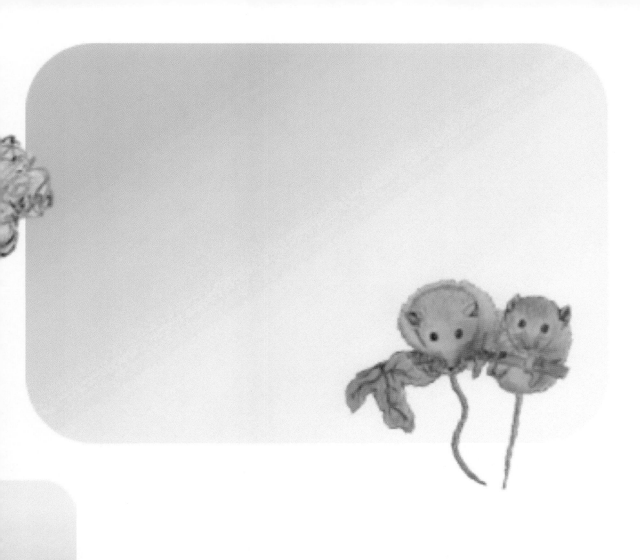

Baby Bear lay back to watch a mother dormouse and her baby climb in the vines.

And Baby
Bear was
very
happy!

Author **Dr. Mark F. Dorgan** has a PhD in Education and spends much of his week with his baby and toddler grandsons. This book is inspired by his second grandson, Raf (2), who loves animals, especially the deer.

Baby Bear Loves Woodland Animals is a book designed to help toddlers from 1-4 years begin to learn the names of common woodland animals in their environment, just as language is emerging and developing.

The **Baby Bear loves...** series. In this series, Baby Bear explores the things in his world that fascinate him, from leaves and flowers, to birds and people. Each title teaches 5 concepts, words or ideas and is suitable for toddlers of 1-4 years of age, just as language is emerging and growing, but before children can write. The illustrations offer strong visual prompts and the adult reader emphasises the words that go with the pictures.

Printed in Great Britain
by Amazon

16797777R00016